Daily Readings with
St Francis of Assisi

The Daily Readings Series
General Editor: Robert Llewelyn

Daily Readings with St Francis of Assisi

Selected and arranged by
Sister Elizabeth Marie Klepec, OSF

With an introduction by
John Garvey

Templegate Publishers
Springfield, Illinois

Arrangement © Templegate Publishers 1988
Introduction © Thomas More Press 1976

ISBN 0-87243-170-3

First published in the United States by
Templegate Publishers
302 East Adams St., P.O. Box 5152
Springfield, Illinois 62705

* * * * * * *

Contents

* * * * * * *

This book is the work of Sister Elizabeth Marie
Klepec, OSF, who has selected and arranged
all the quotations and provided the index of
sources on pages 95 and 96.

All quotations from Franciscan sources are
used with the generous permission of Franciscan Herald Press, Chicago, Illinois.

Introduction

There is probably no saint as appealing to so many people as Francis of Assisi. He has been called the saint who is most like Christ. Even in the wild company of saints his literal acceptance of the Gospel stands out. But much of the appreciation of Francis has been sentimental, and it ignores aspects of his life that are difficult to understand and not very sympathetic. The popular picture of Francis is one of unrelieved pleasantness: he was an advocate of simple living who gathered like-minded Christians around him; he was good to animals, could talk to them and tame them; everyone liked him.

It is true that early accounts of Francis' life stress his attractiveness to many people, people who might have found another person insane if he were to act the way Francis did. And the taming of the wolf of Gubbio and Francis' sermon to the birds are stories that circulated within a couple of generations of the first Franciscans. There must be some truth to the pleasant picture of Francis that has come down to us.

Here, however, we are confronted with the same problem Jesus poses. Our tendency is to look only at the Jesus who was kind to children and sinners, and not the severe Jesus, the one who was quick to expose hypocrisy, drive moneylenders from the temple, whose behavior to his mother and his followers seems at times abrupt, if not rude. However likable Francis was, however tender, there is another and more paradoxical facet of his life that may be more important to an understanding of Francis. It

may be more important because if it is true that
Francis was like Christ, the vital point is not to
emphasize those virtues that everyone understands, but those strange things that almost
nobody understands, and hardly anyone likes.
We love the Francis who was kind, and the
Francis who composed hymns to the sun is
marvelous; but it is hard to feel near to the
Francis who stripped himself naked to show his
independence from his family, or who threw
himself into thorn bushes. Francis was, in
worldly terms, uncompromising and unrealis-
tic. When his followers asked for some of the
security every other religious order knew, he
was furious. Although by the time he died he
was loved by thousands, during the time immediately following his conversion he was considered mad and was beaten by people who
were offended by his rags and his eccentric
behavior.

It is this Francis we must try to understand—
the fool for Christ, who said that the Passion
and humiliation of Jesus were all the instruction
he needed.

The notion of becoming a fool for Christ's
sake goes back to the passage in the Gospel
where Jesus rejoiced that God had revealed his
truth to the simple and had hidden it from those
the world calls wise; and the theme is taken up
by Paul, who calls the Cross a scandal because it
contradicts the wisdom of the world . . . it is folly. John Saward writes (in *The Fool for Christ's
Sake in Monasticism*—1975), "The most important characteristic of the fools, the basis and
inspiration of all that they do and are, is identity

with Christ crucified, their participation in the poverty, nakedness, humiliation, and abandonment of the Lord; and here the spirit of folly for Christ's sake comes close to the spirit of martyrdom." Saward quotes Kologrivov, who writes that the basis of the fool's vocation "is the awareness of the soul's terrible responsibility toward God," a responsibility that consists of "taking voluntarily on oneself humiliations and insults, in order to increase humility, meekness, and kindness of heart, and so to develop love, even for one's enemies and persecutors."

The fool for Christ's sake has appeared again and again in Christian history. In Russia it became a kind of charismatic institution. Saward mentions the fact that Russian fools for Christ usually appeared as pilgrims, who frequently offended the pious. Saint Basil the Blessed stole the merchandise of dishonest tradesmen, stoned the houses of the respectable, wept with sinners, and denounced the injustice of the Czar. He once offered Ivan the Terrible a piece of raw meat; Ivan refused, and Basil then showed him in the sky the souls of innocent people Ivan had murdered. In the West the same phenomenon occurred. Saint Philip Neri shaved half his beard off, wore his coat inside out, walked past the tabernacle without genuflecting; and like Basil he combined this with a sense of social justice, working to prevent Gypsies from being used as galley slaves by the papal fleet. Following his conversion, Saint John of God was considered a lunatic, and there are numerous other examples of this strange way of responding to the Gospel.

Of course we have to consider the possibility that such people really were mad. But as easy as this judgement might be in the case of some saints whose behavior strikes us as outrageous (Christina the Astonishing, for example, whose weird behavior is frankly described as schizophrenic by her most recent Catholic biographers), it doesn't hold up for others. St. Basil's mad behavior before the Czar told a truth that the more restrained sanity of the "respectable" did not dare to tell. The Gospel reveals things hidden from the beginning of time, and the uncovering of those things can lead to strange behavior—Bartimaeus calls out to Jesus for mercy, while his embarrassed companions try to silence him; Zacchaeus climbs a tree to get a glimpse of Jesus, leaving respectability behind. What the world considers crazy makes sense in this context.

It is not possible to retain both our sense of having an easy place in this world and the notion that we are following Christ. Kierkegaard calls the desire to maintain respectability and worldly honor while calling oneself a Christian "wanting to have a mouthful of flour, and blow." Jesus said that his followers were to leave all they had behind, not looking back; he said that following him meant taking up the cross daily, and dying to self. What this means will vary, life to life. But what it does *not* mean is peace, as the world gives it. It does not mean an easy life, or a life that is at home in any society. To the extent that we are willing to serve both God and Mammon, we are not followers of Christ; and we are not, in fact, following God at all. Jesus did not say that it is undesirable to follow God and Mammon. He said you *cannot* do it. What you serve is not God, but an idol of the same name, as long as your allegiance is half-hearted.

It seems to me that the least healthy way to deal with our half-heartedness is to seek a means of making ourselves feel committed without having to change our lives in any but an emotional way, through involvement with enthusiastic group movements that reinforce our belief that we really *are* committed to the following of Jesus; the more sophisticated version of this move is to seek help from the *Zeitgeist,* reading the Gospels in the light of the latest issue of *Psychology Today,* proving to ourselves that we really are O.K. and that our discomfort is merely a matter of conditioning. In either case we are looking toward the preservation of the self we are asked to leave behind. We can't believe that "sell all you have, give it to the poor, and follow me" really means "sell all you have, give it to the poor, and follow me." Here we fall back on Kant's ethical imperative and ask (knowing that there is no real danger of this happening), "What would happen if everyone did that?" But the statement is not addressed to everyone, only to you. That fact is one we fall all over ourselves to avoid.

The response we should make to this impasse is to take some encouragement from the answer of Jesus to his Apostles when they asked, in response to his hard sayings, "Who then can be saved?" He answered that what was impossible for man was possible because of God's mercy.

Some of our dilemma was described by Paul, when he said, "The good I would do, I do not." We believe that we are baptized into Christ's death as well as his Resurrection. Our consciousness of failure may be part of the death we are asked to acknowledge. It becomes fatal only when we stop acknowledging it, or try to justify it.

When Christians stop confessing that they are sinners, unprofitable servants, and to that extent that they are not Christians, the Christian faith ends. Consciousness of sin is in this sense the result of baptism: we are baptized into the death of Christ, who was "made sin for us," as well as his Resurrection. Sin is death, and to acknowledge this is the beginning of freedom from death. This means a ruthless honesty, however. You cannot confess sin in the abstract. When John says that the person who denies that he is a sinner is a liar, he does not mean that our response should be an abstract confession of sin but rather an acknowledgement of the sin that is *really* there; and he associates this with the divine Light, which reveals darkness. Kierkegaard defined the best Christian confession as a confession of the fact that we are not Christians.

The problem with the confession of sins, the acknowledgement of the death into which we are baptized, is that it is meant to lead to life. "Wherever we go we carry with us in our body the death that Jesus died, that in this body also life may reveal itself, the life that Jesus lives. For continually, while still alive, we are being surrendered into the hands of death, for Jesus' sake, so that the life of Jesus also may be revealed in this mortal body of ours" (2 Cor. 4:10-11). The form of this life is something revealed to us not only in the person of Jesus, but also in the lives of those who, like Francis, made deliberate, mad-seeming efforts to break with the world of death. Their foolishness is a measure of how radical the break may have to be; our instinctive reaction against the behavior of the fool for Christ is not necessarily a measure of our sanity, but may be the death-world's way of fighting back.

Before his conversion, Francis was a pleasant young man who was known for his cheerfulness and for his generosity to beggars. When he was about twenty he was imprisoned with a number of others who had been caught up in the battle between the cities of Perugia and Assisi. His imprisonment lasted about one year, and upon his release Francis became dangerously ill. The illness was lengthy, and it may have been the beginning of his conversion. He set out to join the Pope's armies, having bought expensive equipment and clothing, but along the way he met a poor man and felt such compassion for him that he exchanged his own clothes for the other man's rags. Shortly afterward Francis became ill once more. Instead of proceeding to battle, he returned to Assisi, realizing that a change was demanded of him. One day he encountered a leper and at first was horrified. But then his horror at the leper turned around to become a horror at his own revulsion. He embraced the leper, and from that time onward his life turned toward the radical following of the Gospel message.

This incident is one that seemed pivotal to Francis himself. In his *Testament* he wrote, "The Lord God gave me, Francis, this way of doing penance: I was a sinner and found it hard to look at lepers, and the Lord God led me among them, and I was merciful to them. As I left them, what had previously seemed bitter turned into sweetness of body and soul. And then, soon after, I left the world."

Francis began to spend time caring for the ill, giving what he could to the poor; and then came the incident that marked him as a fool for Christ. One day as he prayed in the Church of Saint Damian he heard a voice tell him; "Repair my house, which is falling down." With his usual literalness Francis assumed that this meant the church in which he was praying; so he set about repairing it. Unfortunately, he used some of his father's goods in the process, selling them and offering the proceeds to the poor priest who lived at the church. The priest refused the money, which Francis left lying on a window sill.

Francis' father was understandably angry. When he finally caught Francis (who had retreated for prayer and fasting, and possibly to avoid his father), he took him home forcefully, and kept him locked up there. Francis escaped, returning to Saint Damian's, where his father angrily confronted him with a choice: return home or renounce his inheritance, and return the stolen goods. Francis told his father that he was willing to lose his inheritance, but he insisted that the money received from the sale of his father's goods belonged to the poor. Francis' father tried to take him to court;

Francis refused the authority of a civil tribunal. The Bishop of Assisi therefore became the judge. He told Francis that he should return what he had taken from his father. Francis agreed, and saying, "These clothes also belong to him," he stripped himself naked. He repudiated his father, telling him, "Until now I have called you my father on earth; now I say, 'Our Father, who art in heaven.' " His father went home, angry and extremely distressed, and Francis was given the tunic of a laborer who worked for the bishop. From that day he was in every way "the poor man of Assisi," who depended only on God and the charity of others.

Legend should not blind us to what happened here. Francis' treatment of his father was not fair, in any sense of the word. He had in fact stolen his father's property, he tried to refuse restitution, and his repudiation of his father seems self-dramatizing and insensitive. Forgetting that it is Saint Francis who did these things, we would be inclined to say of a person who behaved this way that he was mad, ungrateful, disrespectful, and unkind.

Singing the praises of God, Francis left the bishop and accepted a life that included abject poverty, beatings, and the ridicule of those who could see only foolishness in his repudiation of his family and his odd habit of repairing churches. He lived by begging. He also began to try to live a literal interpretation of the words of the Gospel, so that when he heard "Provide no gold, silver, or copper to fill your purse, no pack for the road, no second coat, no shoes, no stick," he gave away the few clothes he had begged from others and kept only one shabby coat, which he tied with a rope.

Gradually, the abuse of the townspeople turned to admiration. Francis' charity to the sick and the deformed proved that there was more than eccentricity at work in his life. There were rumors of cures performed by Francis, and a community began to form around him. Men from the region were led by his example to undertake the same life. They joined him, leaving their former comfortable lives for a life of poverty and manual labor; where work could not be found, they were told to "have recourse to the table of the Lord"—which is to say, they were to beg. In his *Testament,* Francis insists upon poverty: "Let the brothers see to it that they do not receive, on any account, churches and houses made for them, if these are not in keeping with holy poverty . . . let them always adhere to these injunctions and live in the world like strangers and pilgrims."

Francis' view of poverty was absolute, and so was his view of self-discipline. He threw himself into a thorn bush when troubled by temptation; he fasted frequently; he insisted upon obedience but at the same time was willing to be rebuked by his followers—in fact he frequently demanded it. When the Order had become established and somewhat respectable, Francis fought unsuccessfully to keep it from becoming attached to property. Many of the friars had come to feel that the absolute poverty and the unproscribed asceticism advocated by Francis should be placed within a more secure framework, one which could include ownership of land and a regulated form of self-denial. Francis was enraged. "My brothers," he said, "the Lord has called me to the way of simplicity and humbleness, and this is the way he has pointed out to me for myself and for those who will believe and follow me. The Lord told me that he would have me poor and foolish in this world, and that he willed not to lead us by any other way than that. May God confound you by your own wisdom and learning and, for all your faultfinding, send you back to your vocation whether you will or not." When some members of the Order wanted to receive official Church recognition for their preaching, in the form of a license from the Pope to preach in every diocese, Francis said that they should live lives that by their holiness would lead bishops to ask the friars for their help. "Let it be your unique privilege to have no privilege," he said.

He did nothing by halves. The *Fioretti* says that when Brother Ruffino did not obey him instantly, Francis, to chastise him, ordered him to preach naked to the people of Assisi. Then, when Ruffino had left, Francis was angry with himself for the harshness of his order and so he too went naked to Assisi, to join Ruffino. The people who saw them assumed they were mad, until they listened to the words of Francis, who "spoke so marvelously of the contempt of the world, of holy penance, of voluntary poverty, of the desire of the heavenly Kingdom, and of the nakedness and humiliation of the passion of our Lord Jesus Christ, that all those present, a great number of men and women, began to weep aloud with great devotion."

What can we make of this extreme behavior, of a man who takes such abrupt leave of his family and refuses to compromise at any point? His father had reason to be angry with him; his friars later found his way of life too demanding, and their desire for some security was certainly reasonable. His behavior was always a bit wild.

First of all, it should be said that the age was in need of a shock. The Church was decadent in the extreme. During the late twelfth and early thirteenth centuries, the time of Francis' life, the Cathar church was making converts—largely because of the corruption of the established Church. The Cathars were dualists, who believed that the world was the creation of a fallen spirit; to be freed from the demonic spirit that ruled the world, to free the divine Light imprisoned in the flesh, severe asceticism was necessary. The Cathar *perfecti*—the closest thing to a Cathar clergy—received a sacrament called the *Consolamentum,* following which they were not allowed to marry or to eat meat. Their fasts were extreme. Their poverty was exemplary. The Cathars combined their ascetic living and voluntary poverty with a compassion for all life, and their kindness to animals was considered unusual. Their teachings were widely accepted in the south of France and the north of Italy, though few Cathar believers felt able to accept the rigors of the life demanded of the *perfecti.* Cathar doctrine was frequently spread by two odd groups of travelers: troubadour poets and weavers.

Although his Catholicism isn't in question—he insisted on his absolute acceptance of Church teaching—Francis' way of life was, in the opinion of many scholars, influenced by Cathar thought. His radical poverty, his extreme asceticism, his feeling for animals, his poetry, his pacifism (he forbade the lay people who joined his Third Order to carry arms for any purpose)—all of these were closer to Cathar thinking than to the conventional Catholic thought of Francis' day. How direct the influence was is impossible to determine, and it is probably best to say that Francis and the Cathars responded to the same set of problems, though Francis' response was a kind of unorthodox orthodoxy, whereas the Cathars (more rule-bound than Francis ever was) were orthodox heretics. In any case, it took a radical effort to understand the Gospel clearly in a time when the Church was both established and decadent. Francis' movement served as a reforming influence, and some have gone so far as to say that if it had been more successful there would never have been a Reformation (though the rise of nationalism and consequent anti-Roman feelings makes this doubtful).

But his major purpose was not reform. Francis simply tried to live what he heard in the Gospel, and the simplicity and wholeheartedness of the attempt made him appear foolish.

It is hard, in any terms that we can understand, to see all of his actions sympathetically. It is better to see in them the literal application of such Gospel counsels as "If anyone comes to me and does not hate his father and mother, wife and children, brothers and sisters, even his own life, he cannot be a disciple of mine. No one who does not carry his cross and come with me can be a disciple of mine." This demand for single-mindedness and total surrender to God led to Francis' repudiation of his father, his obsession with Jesus' Passion, and his definition of obedience: it meant, he said, that you should not be like a dead body. Before words like those of Jesus, and lives like those of Francis, we are uncomfortable. Rather than offer a defense of the words it is important to see the fruits of trying to live them, something the Gospel shows us in the Resurrection and the joy of Pentecost, and the lives of saints show us by revealing a little of the kingdom of God. In Francis' case we find tales of the kingdom in the *Fioretti,* a collection of Franciscan stories that was compiled within a couple of generations of Francis' death. The spirit that informs the *Fioretti* is the spirit of poverty—what it means to leave absolutely everything for the sake of the kingdom of God. The impression is one of sustained ecstasy, and it is sometimes frightening:

St. Francis went behind the altar and began to pray. In that prayer he received a divine visitation that inflamed his soul with such love of holy poverty that from the color of his face and the frequent opening of his mouth it seemed as if flames of fire came from him. Coming toward his companion as if aflame he cried out, "Ah, ah, ah! Brother Masseo, come to me." He repeated this three times, and the third time lifted Brother Masseo into the air with his very breath, and propelled him the distance one could hurl a spear. Brother Masseo . . . later told his companions that when he had been raised by the saint's breath and so softly thrown, he felt such sweetness of soul and consolation of the Holy Spirit as he had never felt before or since.

Stories like this one remind us of something so simple we tend to forget it: God is much stranger than we think. I am reminded of a story repeated by Elie Wiesel in *Souls on Fire* (Random House, 1972) about the son of the Baal Shem who asked his dead father in a dream,

"How can I serve God?" The Baal Shem climbed a high mountain and threw himself into the abyss. "Like this," he answered. Another time the Baal Shem appeared to him as a mountain on fire, erupting into a thousand flaming fragments: "And like this as well."

Wiesel relates another story, one close to the story of Brother Masseo:

"One day," Rebbe Wolfe of Zhitomir tells us, "we were all sitting around the table in the House of Study. It was a Friday afternoon. We could hear the Maggid, in his study next door, reading the Sidra, the weekly portion of Scripture customarily read on Shabbat. Suddenly he stopped, the door opened, and there he was, standing motionless in the doorway, staring at us, or perhaps at something beyond us. His whole being was on fire, but most of all, his face, most of all, his eyes. Seized with panic, Rebbe Pinhas, Rebbe Shmelke, Rebbe Elimelekh, and Rebbe Zusia ran into the street. Rebbe Levi-Yitzhak hid under the table. As for me, gripped by a strange exultation, I began to applaud with all my strength—and to this day I regret it."

These stories come from the Hasidic tradition, a Jewish movement that has much in common with Franciscanism, including tales of conversion, enthusiasm, asceticism, and ecstasy. They remind us that God is not an idea, a static being toward whom we aspire, but instead is a fire. From the burning bush, God gave his name to Moses: I am. And that Being was not a metaphysical notion but a fire that burns without consuming. That fire led to the ecstasy known by one of Francis' first followers, Brother Giovanni, who was so given over to God that at times when he would hear his master speak of God, his heart would melt like wax near a fire; and the love of God so inflamed him that he was not able to stand still and endure it. He would get up and, as if drunk in spirit, would go about now through the garden, now through the woods, now through the church, talking as the flame and the impetus of the spirit moved him.

Brother Masseo, after a period of torment, was given such a joyful humility that

frequently when in prayer he would make a steady jubilant sound, like a soft dove. . . . When asked by Brother Jacopo de Fallerone why he never changed the tone of his rejoicing, he answered with great joy that when something goes well there is no need to change it.

The ecstatic element of Franciscan spirituality is balanced by a deep sense of compassion and mercy. One young friar, on seeing that a criminal had been sentenced by a harsh mayor to have his eyes put out, "asked that one eye be taken from him and the other from the evildoer, so that the criminal would not be completely deprived of his sight. The mayor and the council, seeing the fervent charity of the friar, pardoned both him and the criminal."

The Franciscan approach to life takes us to what we would normally regard as extremes: extremes of charity, of asceticism, of ecstasy, and certainly extremes of behavior. The madness involved in being a fool for Christ could have to do with the words of Scripture: that no one can look upon the face of God and live. There is a story told by the Hasidim about four men who made their way into the presence of God. One upon seeing God went mad, another died, another lost his faith, and only one survived intact. A clear sense of God could so unmoor a person from ordinary allegiances, ordinary behavior, that he might seem genuinely insane to us. But the insanity of a Francis is more sane than our caution, and his concentration on the death of Christ is more life-giving than our pursuit of self-fulfillment. The medieval fascination with Jesus' suffering has been criticized by a number of commentators, who point out that where Eastern Christianity emphasizes the Transfiguration, Western Christians emphasize the stigmata and the Passion.

Finally it is all one. The Russian Church, with its transfigured saints, saw a great mystery in the humiliated Christ. Our culture is puritanical about suffering and forgets that it is not a Christian obsession but a permanent reality. It is the beginning of Buddha's revelation, and Plato said that the love of wisdom meant learning how to die. Francis received the stigmata, but the Resurrection and the Transfiguration are there. The *Fioretti* speaks of Francis transfigured, so that "his five stigmata were as five beautiful stars and so radiant that they lit the entire palace with their rays." Reading the *Fioretti*—especially at points like this one—we feel a certain embarrassment, as if we had outgrown that kind of story. But learning to read that kind of story "with eyes that can see" might be the most important task for modern Christians, who should not be embarrassed by this any more than they are by the miracle of loaves and fishes multiplied, or water changed to wine.

John Garvey

THE CRUCIFIX OF SAN DAMIANO WHICH
SPOKE TO SAINT FRANCIS

It is now in Santa Chiara, Assisi.

Who Are You, God, And Who Am I?

Who Are You, God, and Who am I?

My God and my all! Who are you, O God most dear, and who am I, your worthless, useless little worm of a servant!

* * *

What a person is in the eyes of God, so much he is, and no more.

* * *

To myself I seem to be the greatest of sinners, for if God had pursued a criminal with the same mercy, that person would be ten times more spiritual than I.

* * *

Just as in a picture of our Lord or the Blessed Virgin painted on wood our Lord and the Blessed Virgin are honored and yet the wood and the painting ascribe nothing of it to themselves, so is the servant of God a kind of painting of God in which God is honored for his benefaction, but the servant ought to attribute nothing to himself, because in comparison with God he is even less than wood or painting, indeed he is pure nothing.

So, to God alone the honor and glory should be given, to oneself however nothing but shame and tribulation so long as he lives in this world.

A Little Less Than the Angels

Try to realize the dignity God has conferred on you. He created and formed your body in the image of his beloved Son, and your soul in his own likeness (Gen. 1:26). And yet every creature under heaven serves and acknowledges and obeys its Creator in its own way better than you do. Even the devils were not solely responsible for crucifying him; it was you who crucified him with them and continue to crucify him by taking pleasure in your vices and sins.

What have you to be proud of? If you were so clever and learned that you knew everything and could speak every language, so that the things of heaven were an open book to you, still you could not boast of that. Any of the devils knew more about the things of heaven, and knows more about the things of earth, than any human being, even one who might have received from God a special revelation of the highest wisdom. If you were the most handsome and the richest person in the world, and could work wonders and drive out devils, all that would be something extrinsic to you; it would not belong to you and you could not boast of it. But there is one thing of which we can all boast; we can boast of our humiliations (2 Cor. 12:15) and in taking up daily the holy cross of our Lord Jesus Christ.

The Moment of Conversion

This is how God inspired me, Brother Francis, to embark upon a life of penance. When I was in sin, the sight of lepers nauseated me beyond measure; but then God himself led me into their company, and I had pity on them. When I had once become acquainted with them, what had previously nauseated me became a source of spiritual and physical consolation for me. After that I did not wait long before leaving the world.

And God inspired me with such faith in his churches that I used to pray with all simplicity, saying, "We adore you, Lord Jesus Christ, here and in all your churches in the whole world, and we bless you, because by your holy cross you have redeemed the world."

Called To Be Servant

It is not for us to be wise and calculating in the world's fashion; we should be guileless, lowly, and pure. We should hold our lower nature in contempt, as a source of shame to us, because through our own fault we are wretched and utterly corrupt, nothing more than worms, as our Lord tells us by the Prophet, *I am a worm, not a man; the scorn of men, despised by the people* (Ps. 21:7). We should not want to be in charge of others; we are to be servants, and should *be subject to every human creature for God's sake* (1 Pet. 2:13). On all those who do this and endure to the last the Spirit of God will rest (Is. 11:2); he will make his dwelling in them and there he will stay, and they will be *children of your Father in heaven* (Mt. 5:45) whose work they do. It is they who are the brides, the brothers and the mothers of our Lord Jesus Christ. A person is his bride when his faithful soul is united with Jesus Christ by the Holy Spirit; we are his brothers and sisters when we do the will of his Father who is in heaven (Mt. 12:50), and we are mothers to him when we enthrone him in our hearts and souls by love with a pure and sincere conscience, and give him birth by doing good. This, too, should be an example to others.

My Worth is Found in God Alone

The Apostle says, *Nobody can say, Jesus is the Lord, except in the Holy Spirit* (1 Cor. 12:3), and it says, *There is no one that does anything good, no, not one* (Ps. 52:4).

So it is that whoever envies another for the good which the Lord says or does in him, comes close to the sin of blasphemy, because his envy touches the Most High, since it is he who says and does what is good.

* * *

Blessed is the servant that does not think himself any the better when people make much of him and exalt him than when they consider him worthless, ordinary, and contemptible. For what a person is before God, so much he is, and no more.

Woe to that one that is elevated by others and is of no mind to get down from his rank of his own accord. And blessed is the servant who is elevated through no will of his own and is always minded to keep at the feet of the rest.

True Poverty of Spirit

Blessed are the poor in spirit, for theirs is the kingdom of heaven (Mt. 5:3). There are many people who spend all their time at their prayers and other religious exercises and mortify themselves by long fasts and so on. But if anyone says as much as a word that implies a reflection on their self-esteem or takes something from them, they are immediately up in arms and annoyed. These people are not really poor in spirit. A person is really poor in spirit when he hates himself and loves those who strike him in the face (Mt. 5:30).

* * *

Blessed is the servant that is no more elated at the good which the Lord says and does through him than at that which he says and does through anybody else.

It is sinful of a person to be more set on receiving from his neighbor than he is willing to give of himself to the Lord God.

Nothing Do I Own

We must be firmly convinced that we have nothing of our own, except our vices and sins. And so we should be glad when we *fall into various trials* (Jam. 1:2), and when we suffer anguish of soul or body, or affliction of any kind in this world, for the sake of life eternal. We must all be on our guard against pride and empty boasting and beware of worldly or natural wisdom. A worldly spirit loves to talk a lot but do nothing, striving for the exterior signs of holiness that people can see, with no desire for true piety and interior holiness of spirit. It was about people like this that our Lord said, *Amen I say to you, they have received their reward* (Mt. 6:2). The spirit of God, on the other hand, inspires us to mortify and despise our lower nature and regard it as a source of shame, worthless and of no value. Humility, patience, perfect simplicity, and true peace of heart are all its aim, but above everything else it desires the fear of God, the divine wisdom and the divine love of the Father, Son, and Holy Spirit.

Bound To Captivity

All those who refuse to do penance and receive the Body and Blood of our Lord Jesus Christ are blind, because they cannot see the true light, our Lord Jesus Christ. They indulge their vices and sins and follow their evil longings and desires, without a thought for the promises they made. In body they are slaves of the world and of the desires of their lower nature, with all the cares and anxieties of this life; in spirit they are slaves of the devil. They have been led astray by him and have made themselves his children, dedicated to doing his work. They lack spiritual insight because the Son of God does not dwell in them, and it is he who is the true wisdom of the Father. It is of such as these that scripture says, *their skill was swallowed up* (Ps. 106:27). They can see clearly and are well aware what they are doing; they are fully conscious of the fact that they are doing evil, and knowingly lose their souls.

As Gold Is Tried By Fire

Do not be afraid because you are tempted. The more you are beset by temptation, the greater servant and friend of God do I consider you. I tell you that nobody in fact ought to consider himself a perfect friend of God except insofar as he passes through many trials and temptations.

* * *

A temptation vanquished is, so to say, the ring with which the Lord espouses to himself the soul of his servant. Many there are who flatter themselves on merits of years' standing and feel happy at having undergone no temptations. They should know that because the fright of it alone, previous to the clash, would overwhelm them, their weakness of spirit was taken into account by the Lord. Vigorous contests are scarcely put up to people except where their ability has been perfected.

* * *

Overgreat security leads to lessened caution against the enemy. If the Devil can get hold of a single hair of a person, he soon has it enlarged to a cable. And if for years on end he is not able to down the person he has been tempting, he does not haggle over the delay so long as the person gives in to him in the end. That is his business. He thinks of nothing else day and night.

God's Mercy Restores Joy

Why do you show your sorrow and sadness for your sins exteriorly? Keep such sadness between yourself and God, and pray that in his mercy he may pardon you and give back to your soul the gladness of his salvation of which it has been deprived by the demerit of sin. But before me and the rest try always to have a cheerful air; it does not become a servant of God to appear before anybody else with sadness and a troubled countenance.

* * *

If the servant of God studies to have and keep, within and without, that spiritual cheerfulness which proceeds from a clean heart and is acquired by devotion to prayer, the evil spirits cannot harm him . . . But the demons are elated when they can extinguish or in a measure interfere with the devotion and joy proceeding from prayer that is pure, and from other virtuous actions.

Restore the Joy of My Salvation, Lord

The Devil exults most when he can steal a person's joy of spirit from him. He carries a powder with him to throw into any smallest possible chinks of our conscience, to soil the spotlessness of our mind and the purity of our life. But when spiritual joy fills our hearts, the Serpent pours out his deadly poison in vain.

The demons cannot hurt a servant of Christ when they see him filled with holy mirth. But when his spirit is tearful, forlorn, downcast, it is readily swallowed up completely by sadness, or it is carried to the extreme of vain enjoyments . . . When a servant of God, as commonly happens, is troubled about anything, he ought to get right up and pray, and insist on staying in his sovereign Father's presence until he restores the joy of his salvation to him. For if he lingers in his gloom, that Babylonian mess will ripen to the point where, if not flushed out with tears, it will generate permanent corrosion in the heart.

The Praise of the Virtues I

Hail, Queen Wisdom! The Lord save you,
    with your sister, pure, holy Simplicity.
Lady Holy Poverty, God keep you,
    with your sister, holy Humility.
Lady Holy Love, God keep you,
    with your sister, holy Obedience.
All holy virtues,
    God keep you,
    God, from whom you proceed and come.
In all the world there is not a person
    who can possess any one of you
    without first dying to himself.
The person who practices one and does not
offend against the others
    possesses all;
The person who offends against one
    possesses none and violates all.
Each and every one of you
    puts vice and sin to shame.
Holy Wisdom puts Satan
    and all his wiles to shame.
Pure and holy Simplicity puts
    all the learning of this world,
    all natural wisdom, to shame.

The Praise of the Virtues II

Holy Poverty puts to shame
    all greed, avarice,
    and all the anxieties of this life.
Holy Humility puts pride to shame,
    and all the inhabitants of this world
    and all that is in the world.
Holy Love puts to shame all the temptations
    of the devil and the flesh
    and all natural fear.
Holy Obedience puts to shame
    all natural and selfish desires.
It mortifies our lower nature
    and makes it obey the spirit
    and our brothers and sisters.
Obedience subjects a person
    to everyone on earth,
And not only to people,
    but to all the beasts as well
    and to the wild animals,
So that they can do what they like with him,
    as far as God allows them.

Embrace of Virtues

Where there is charity and wisdom,
   there is neither fear nor ignorance.
Where there is patience and humility,
   there is neither anger nor loss of composure.
Where there is poverty borne with joy,
   there is neither grasping nor hoarding.
Where there is quiet and meditation,
   there is neither worry nor dissipation.
Where there is the fear of the Lord to guard
the gateway,
   there the Enemy can get no hold for an
   entry.
Where there is mercy and discernment,
   there is neither luxury nor a hardened heart.

What Is It You Want Me To Do,

ord?

Discerning God's Will

O great God of glory, my Lord Jesus Christ,
I entreat you, put light into the darkness of
    my mind.
Give me the right faith, firm hope, and perfect
    charity.
Help me learn to know you, O Lord, so well
    that in all things
I may do everything in true keeping
    with your holy will.

              * * *

Almighty, eternal, just and merciful God, grant
us in our misery that we may do for your sake
alone what we know you want us to do, and
always want what pleases you; so that, cleansed
and enlightened interiorly and fired with the ar-
dour of the Holy Spirit, we may be able to
follow in the footsteps of your Son, our Lord
Jesus Christ, and so make our way to you, Most
High, by your grace alone, you who live and
reign in perfect Trinity and simple Unity, and
are glorified, God all powerful, for ever and
ever. Amen.

Humbly Receive the Word of God

St. Paul tells us, *The letter kills, but the spirit gives life* (2 Cor. 3:6). A person has been killed by the letter when he wants to know quotations only so that people will think he is very learned and he can make money to give to his relatives and friends. A person has been killed by the letter when he has no desire to follow the spirit of Sacred Scripture, but wants only to know what it says only so that he can explain it to others. On the other hand, those have received life from the spirit of Sacred Scripture who, by their words and example, refer to the most high God, to whom belongs all good, all that they know or wish to know, and do not allow their knowledge to become a source of self-complacency.

Jesus Christ Teaches Me

It is good to read what Scripture testifies, good to seek out our Lord in it. For my part, I have fixed in mind so much of the Scriptures that it now suffices most amply for my meditation and reflection. I do not need very much, my son: I know about poor Christ crucified!

* * *

Look at the Good Shepherd, my brothers. To save his sheep he endured the agony of the cross. They followed him in trials and persecutions, in ignominy, hunger, and thirst, in humiliations and temptations. And for this God rewarded them with eternal life. We ought to be ashamed of ourselves; the saints endured all that, but we who are servants of God try to win honor and glory by recounting and making known what they have done.

He Emptied Himself

Our Lord Jesus Christ is the glorious Word of
the Father, so holy and exalted, whose coming
the Father made known by St. Gabriel the Archangel to the glorious and blessed Virgin Mary, in
whose womb he took on our weak human
nature. He was rich beyond measure and yet he
and his holy Mother chose poverty.

* * *

Now, such was the will of his Father that his
glorious blest Son, whom he gave up to us and
who was born for us, should offer himself up in
his own blood as a sacrifice and victim on the
altar of the cross, not for himself, through
whom all things have been made (Jn. 1:3), but
for our sins, leaving us an example, so that we
might follow in his footsteps (1 Pet. 2:21). It is
his will that we all should be saved by him and
receive him with a pure heart and a chaste body.
But there are few who care to receive him and
be saved by him, though his yoke is sweet and
his burden light (Mt. 11:30).

He Held Nothing Back

. . . God's only begotten Son, who is the supreme Wisdom, descended from the bosom of the Father for the salvation of souls in order to instruct the world by his example and speak the word of salvation to the people, whom he was both to redeem with the price and cleanse with the bath and nourish with the drink of his sacred Blood, keeping nothing whatever back for himself that he did not give away liberally for our salvation. And since we ought to do everything according to the model of what we see in him as on a high mountain, it seems to be more pleasing to God for me to interrupt my retirement and go out for such work.

My Lady Poverty

I *am* going to marry a bride, one nobler and
fairer than any you have ever seen, one that will
be outstanding for beauty and will impress
everybody else for wit.

* * *

It is poverty which makes people heirs and
kings of the Kingdom of Heaven, not your false
riches.

* * *

Understand that poverty is a choice way of
salvation; the fruit it bears is manifold, and rare
are they who know it well.

* * *

Blessed is the servant that returns all the goods
he has to the Lord God.

For whoever withholds anything for himself,
hides away his Lord's money on his own person
(Mt. 25:18), and so, what he thinks he has, will
be taken from him (Lk. 8:18).

The Lord Gave Me Brothers

And after the Lord gave me some brothers, there was nobody to show me what to do; but the Most High himself revealed to me that I was to live according to the form of the Holy Gospel. And I caused it to be written down simply and in a few words, and the Lord Pope approved it for me. And those who came to take up this life, gave all they could possess to the poor, and they were content with one tunic patched inside and out if they wished, besides a cincture and drawers. And we wished to have nothing else.

* * *

If you want to join the poor of God, first distribute your goods to the poor.

* * *

Brothers, let us begin to serve God our Lord, for up till now we have made little or no progress.

God Chooses the Least

Do you want to know why everybody is following me? That is happening to me because of the eyes of God on high taking in everywhere the good and the bad. Those most holy eyes have espied nobody among sinners more useless, incompetent, and sinful than I, and to do the marvels he has in mind, he has found no more worthless creature on earth. And so he has chosen me, to put to shame what is noble and grand and powerful and fair and wise about the world, so that it may be clear that all virtue and all that is good comes from him and not from any creature; and no person may glory in his sight, but whoever glories, shall glory in the Lord, to whom be all the honor and glory forever.

In Defense of Poverty

For the Lord takes great pleasure in poverty, especially in the form of voluntary begging, while I possess a regal dignity and a distinguished nobility when I imitate the Lord who, rich as he was, became poor for our sake. . . . I get more satisfaction out of a poor table set with little alms than out of grand tables with almost countless dishes.

* * *

If we owned anything, we should have to have weapons to protect ourselves. That is what gives rise to contentions and lawsuits, and so often causes the love of God and neighbor to be interfered with. For ourselves, we are resolved to possess nothing temporal in this world.

Vanity of Vanities

Our Lord tells us in the Gospel, *Take heed and guard yourselves from all covetousness* (Lk. 12:15) and malice; and *Take heed of the cares of this life* (Lk. 21:34) and the anxieties of the world. And so all the friars, no matter where they are or where they go, are forbidden to take or accept money in any way or under any form, or have it accepted for them, for clothing or books, or as wages, or in any other necessity, except to provide for the urgent needs of those who are ill. We should have no more use or regard for money in any of its forms than for dust. Those who think it is worth more or who are greedy for it, expose themselves to the danger of being deceived by the devil. We have left everything we had behind us; we must be very careful now not to lose the kingdom of heaven for so little. If ever we find money somewhere, we should think no more of it than of the dust we trample under our feet, for it is vanity of vanities, and all vanity (Eccles. 1:2).

The Blessing of Work

Those of us who were clerics said the Office like other clerics, while the lay brothers said the *Our Father,* and we were only too glad to find shelter in abandoned churches. We made no claim to learning and we were submissive to everyone. I worked with my own hands and I am still determined to work; and with all my heart I want all the other friars to be busy with some kind of work that can be carried on without scandal. Those who do not know how to work should learn, not because they want to get something for their efforts, but to give good example and to avoid idleness. When we receive no recompense for our work, we can turn to God's table and beg alms from door to door. God revealed a form of greeting to me, telling me that we should say, "God give you peace."

The Freedom of True Poverty

Let us go to St. Peter and St. Paul, and ask them to teach us and help us get possession of the measureless treasure of holy poverty; for it is a treasure so exceedingly valuable that we are unfit to hold it in the base vessels we are. It is that heavenly virtue by which all earthly transitory things are trodden under foot and every hindrance is removed from the soul, so that it can commune freely with the eternal God. It helps the soul while still on earth to converse with the angels in heaven, it was the companion of Christ on the Cross, it was buried with Christ, it rose again with Christ, and with Christ it ascended into heaven. It is the virtue, too, which renders their flight to heaven easy for those who love it. It protects us with the armor of true humility and charity.

The Humility of Jesus in the Crib and the Eucharist

If you wish us to celebrate the festival of our Lord at Greccio, hurry on ahead and prepare exactly what I am telling you. For I want to observe the memory of that Child who was born at Bethlehem, and in some way see before my bodily eyes the discomforts of his baby needs, how he was laid there in the manger, and how, with the ox and the ass standing by, he was placed there on the hay.

* * *

Our whole being should be seized with fear, the whole world should tremble and heaven rejoice, when Christ the Son of the living God is present on the altar in the hands of the priest. What wonderful majesty! What stupendous condescension! O sublime humility! O humble sublimity! That the Lord of the whole universe, God and the Son of God, should humble himself like this and hide under the form of a little bread for our salvation. Look at God's condescension, my sisters and brothers, and *pour out your hearts before him* (Ps. 61:9). Humble yourselves that you may be exalted by him (1 Pet. 5:6). Keep nothing for yourselves, so that he who has given himself wholly to you may receive you wholly.

Be Not Dull Of Heart But Believe

. . . Why do you refuse to recognize the truth *and believe in the Son of God?* (Jn. 9:35). Every day he humbles himself just as he did when he came from his *heavenly throne* (Wis. 18:15) into the Virgin's womb; every day he comes to us and lets us see him in abjection, when he descends from the bosom of the Father into the hands of the priest at the altar. He shows himself to us in this sacred bread just as he once appeared to his apostles in real flesh. With their own eyes they saw only his flesh, but they believed that he was God, because they contemplated him with the eyes of the spirit. We, too, with our own eyes, see only bread and wine, but we must see further and firmly believe that this is his most holy Body and Blood, living and true. In this way our Lord remains continually with his followers, as he promised, *Behold, I am with you all days, even unto the consummation of the world* (Mt. 28:20).

Receive the Eucharist with Faith

And so now, with all those who see the Blessed
Sacrament, sanctified by our Lord's words on
the altar, through the hands of the priest, in the
form of bread and wine: if they do not see and
believe, as the spirit and the Divine nature demand, that it is truly the most holy Body and
Blood of our Lord Jesus Christ, they stand con-
demned. For it is the Most High who bears
witness to it. He says, *This is my body, and the
blood of the New Testament* (Mk. 14:22-24)
and, *He who eats my flesh and drinks my
blood, has life everlasting* (Jn. 6:55).

Thus it is the spirit of the Lord, which dwells in
those who believe in him, that truly receives the
most holy Body and Blood of our Lord. All the
rest, who have nothing of that spirit and
presume to receive him, eat and drink judgement to themselves (1 Cor. 11:29).

Awesome Respect for the Ordained Priest

God inspired me, too, and still inspires me with such great faith in priests . . . because of their dignity, that if they persecuted me, I should still be ready to turn to them for aid. And if I were as wise as Solomon and met the poorest priests of the world, I would still refuse to preach against their will in the parishes in which they live. I am determined to reverence, love and honour priests and all others as my superiors. I refuse to consider their sins, because I can see the Son of God in them and they are better than I. I do this because in this world I cannot see the most high Son of God with my own eyes, except for his most holy Body and Blood which they receive and they alone administer to others.

* * *

If I were at the same time to meet some saint coming down from Heaven and any poor little priest, I would first pay my respects to the priest and proceed to kiss his hands first. I would say, "Ah, just a moment, St. Lawrence, because this person's hands handle the Word of Life and possess something that is more than human."

Am The Herald Of The Great King

Mission to the World

I am the herald of the Great King.

* * *

We Friars Minor, servants and worthless as we are, humbly beg and implore everyone to persevere in the true faith and in a life of penance; there is no other way to be saved. We beseech the whole world to do this, all those who serve our Lord and God within the holy, catholic, and apostolic Church, together with the whole hierarchy, priests, deacons, subdeacons, acolytes, exorcists, lectors, porters, and clerics and religious, male or female; we beg all children, big and small, the poor and the needy, kings and princes, labourers and farmers, servants and masters; we beg all virgins and all other women, married or unmarried; we beg all lay folk, men and women, infants and adolescents, young and old, the healthy and the sick, the little and the great, all peoples, tribes, families and languages, all nations and all people everywhere, present and to come; we Friars Minor beg them all to persevere in the true faith and in a life of penance.

Go, and Preach to All Nations

Listen, then, sons of God and my friars, and *give ear to my words* (Acts 2:14). Give hearing (Is. 55:3) with all your hearts and obey the voice of the Son of God. Keep his commandments wholeheartedly and practise his counsels with all your minds. *Give thanks to the Lord, for he is good* (Ps. 135:1); *extol him in your works* (Tob. 13:6). This is the very reason he has sent you all over the world, so that by word and deed you might bear witness to his message and convince everyone *that there is no other almighty God besides him* (Tob. 13:4). Be well disciplined then and patient under holy obedience, keeping your promises to him generously and unflinchingly. *God deals with you as with sons* (Heb. 12:7).

Preach Patience And Live It

You cannot tell what degree of patience and humility a servant of God has about him as long as he has been having his way.

But let the time come when those who should oblige him, do the contrary to him, and what degree of patience and humility he has then, that is the degree he has and no more.

* * *

Blessed is the person that puts up with the frailty of his neighbor to the extent he would like his neighbor to put up with him if he were in a similar plight.

* * *

Blessed is the servant that takes direction, blame, and reproof as patiently from anyone else as from himself.

Blessed is the servant that on being reproved cheerfully agrees, modestly complies, humbly confesses, and readily makes amends.

Blessed is the servant that is not quick to excuse himself, and humbly accepts the embarrassment and the reproof for a sin where he was not guilty of any fault.

But I Say to You, Love Your Enemies

Our Lord says in the Gospel: *Love your enemies* (Mt. 5:44).

That person truly loves his enemy who does not grieve over the injury done to himself, but for the love of God is on fire over the sin on the person's soul and proceeds to show his love for him by his actions.

* * *

Remember the words of our Lord, *Love your enemies, do good to those who hate you* (Mt. 5:44). Our Lord Jesus Christ himself, in whose footsteps we must follow (1 Pet. 2:21), called the man who betrayed him his friend, and gave himself up of his own accord to his executioners. Therefore, our friends are those who for no reason cause us trouble and suffering, shame or injury, pain or torture, even martyrdom and death. It is these we must love, and love very much, because for all they do to us we are given eternal life.

Exercising Authority With Mercy

Let any person, however, who is entrusted with the obedience of others and who is regarded as someone greater, become like someone lesser (Lk. 22:26) and like the servant of the rest of the brethren, and let him have and show his several brethren, the mercy he would wish to have done to himself in any similar case. And let him not get angry with a person over the offense of another, but kindly admonish him and bear with him with all patience and humility.

* * *

Those who have been entrusted with the power of judging others should pass judgement mercifully, just as they themselves hope to obtain mercy from God. *For judgement is without mercy to him who has not shown mercy* (James 2:13). We must be charitable, too, and humble, and give alms, because they wash the stains of sin from our souls. We lose everything which we leave behind us in this world; we can bring with us only the right to a reward for our charity and the alms we have given. For these we shall receive a reward, a just retribution from God.

Love Has No Exceptions

Blessed is the one that would love another in illness, when he cannot be of use to him, as much as he loves him in health, when he can be of use to him.

Blessed is the one that would love and respect another if he were far away as much as if he were with him, and would say nothing about him behind his back that in all charity he could not say in his presence.

* * *

Blessed is that one that takes no pleasure and delight except in the very holy things our Lord said and did, and uses them to lead people to cheerful and happy love of God.

And woe to that one that finds his delight in idle and frivolous talk and makes use of it to make people laugh.

* * *

Nothing should upset a person except sin. And even then, no matter what kind of sin has been committed, if he is upset or angry for any other reason except charity, he is only drawing blame upon himself. A person lives a good life and avoids sin when he is never angry or disturbed at anything. Blessed the one who keeps nothing for himself, but renders *to Caesar the things that are Caesar's, and to God the things that are God's* (Mt. 22:21).

Live the Peace You Preach

The Lord revealed to me that we should speak this greeting: The Lord give you peace.

* * *

Blessed are the peacemakers, for they shall be called the children of God (Mt. 5:9). They are truly peacemakers who are able to preserve their peace of mind and heart for love of our Lord Jesus Christ, despite all that they suffer in this world.

* * *

While you are proclaiming peace with your lips, be careful to have it even more fully in your heart. Nobody should be roused to wrath or insult on your account. Everyone should rather be moved to peace, goodwill and mercy as a result of your self-restraint.

For we have been called for the purpose of healing the wounded, binding up those who are bruised, and reclaiming the erring. Many a person may seem to us a child of the Devil that will one day be a disciple of Christ.

Peace Prayer of St. Francis

Lord, make me an instrument of your peace;
   where there is hatred, let me sow love;
   where there is injury, pardon;
   where there is doubt, faith;
   where there is despair, hope;
   where there is darkness, light;
   and where there is sadness, joy.

O Divine Master, grant that I may not so much
seek
      to be consoled as to console,
      to be understood as to understand,
      to be loved as to love.

   For it is in giving that we receive;
      it is in pardoning that we are pardoned;
      and it is in dying that we are born to
      eternal life.

My

od
And My All

Praises of God

You are holy, Lord, the only God,
  and your deeds are wonderful.
You are strong,
  You are great.
  You are the Most High,
  You are almighty.
  You, holy Father, are
  King of heaven and earth.
You are Three and One,
  Lord God, all good,
  You are Good, all Good, supreme Good,
  Lord God, living and true.
You are love,
  You are wisdom.
  You are humility,
  You are endurance.
  You are rest,
  You are peace.
  You are joy and gladness.
  You are justice and moderation.
  You are all our riches,
  And you suffice for us.
You are beauty.
  You are gentleness.
  You are our protector,
  You are our guardian and defender.
  You are courage.
  You are our haven and our hope.
You are our faith,
  Our great consolation.
  You are our eternal life,
  Great and wonderful Lord,
  God almighty,
  Merciful Saviour.

In Praise of a Loving God

How glorious, how holy and wonderful it is to have a Father in heaven. How holy it is, how beautiful and lovable to have in heaven a Bridegroom. How holy and beloved, how pleasing and lowly, how peaceful, delightful, lovable and desirable above all things it is to have a Brother like this, who laid down his life for his sheep (Jn. 10:15), and prayed to his Father for us, saying: Holy Father, in your name keep those whom you have given me. Father, all those whom you gave me in the world, were yours and you gave them to me. And the words you have given me, I have given to them. And they have received them and have known truly that I have come forth from you, and they have believed that you have sent me. I am praying for them, not for the world; bless and sanctify them. And for them I sanctify myself, that they may be sanctified in their unity, just as we are. And, Father, I wish that where I am, they also may be with me, that they may see my splendour in your kingdom (Jn. 17:6-24).

* * *

Well deserving of our love is the love of him who loved us so well.

Our God, Worthy of All Praise

We should wish for nothing else and have no other desire; we should find no pleasure or delight in anything except in our Creator, Redeemer, and Saviour; he alone is true God, who is perfect good, all good, every good, the true and supreme good, and he alone is good, loving and gentle, kind and understanding; he alone is holy, just, true, and right; he alone is kind, innocent, pure, and from him, through him, and in him is all pardon, all grace, and all glory for the penitent, the just, and the blessed who rejoice in heaven.

Nothing, then, must keep us back, nothing separate us from him, nothing come between us and him. At all times and seasons, in every country and place, every day and all day, we must have a true and humble faith, and keep him in our hearts, where we must love, honour, adore, serve, praise and bless, glorify and acclaim, magnify and thank, the most high supreme and eternal God, Three and One, Father, Son, and Holy Spirit, Creator of all and Saviour of those who believe in him, who hope in him, and who love him; without beginning and without end, he is unchangeable, invisible, indescribable and ineffable, incomprehensible, unfathomable, blessed and worthy of all praise, glorious, exalted, sublime, most high, kind, lovable, delightful and utterly desirable beyond all else, for ever and ever.

Praising the All-Good

Every creature in heaven and on earth and in the depths of the sea, give God praise and glory and honour and blessing (Ap. 5:13); he has borne so much for us and has done and will do so much good to us; he is our power and our strength, and he alone is good (Lk. 18:19), he alone most high, he alone all-powerful, wonderful, and glorious; he alone is holy and worthy of all praise and blessing for endless ages and ages. Amen.

* * *

Almighty, most holy, most high and sovereign God, the sovereign good, everything that is good, wholly good, who alone are good: to you let us render all praise, all glory, all thanks, all honour, all blessing, and to you let us refer always whatever is good. Amen.

* * *

We must refer every good to the most high supreme God, acknowledging that all good belongs to him; and we must thank him for it all, because all good comes from him. May the most supreme and high and only true God receive and have and be paid all honour and reverence, all praise and blessing, all thanks and all glory, for to him belongs all good and *no one is good but only God* (Lk. 18:19). And when we see or hear people speaking or doing evil or blaspheming God, we must say and do good, praising God, who is blessed for ever.

We Give You Thanks, O God

Almighty, most high and supreme God, Father, holy and just, Lord, King of heaven and earth, we give you thanks for yourself. Of your own holy will you created all things spiritual and physical, made us in your own image and likeness, and gave us a place in paradise, through your only Son, in the Holy Spirit. And it was through our own fault that we fell. We give you thanks because, having created us through your Son, by that holy love with which you loved us, you decreed that he should be born, true God and true man, of the glorious and ever blessed Virgin Mary and redeem us from our captivity by the blood of his passion and death. We give you thanks because your Son is to come a second time in the glory of his majesty and cast the damned, who refused to do penance and acknowledge you, into everlasting fire; while to all those who acknowledged you, adored you, and served you by a life of penance, he will say: *Come, blessed of my Father, take possession of the kingdom prepared for you from the foundation of the world* (Mt. 25:34).

Unction in Prayer: a Gift of God

When a servant of God is visited by the Lord with some fresh consolation while at prayer, before leaving his prayers he ought to raise his eyes to heaven and say to the Lord with folded hands: You have, O Lord, sent unworthy sinful me this consolation and sweetness from Heaven, and I commit it back to you to save it for me, for I am a thief when it comes to your treasure . . . Lord, take your good gift from me in this world, and save it for me in the world to come.

That is what he ought to do; so that when he comes away from prayer, he will appear to others as much a poor sinful person as if he had not gained any further grace . . . It happens that an invaluable thing is lost at a cheap price; and that easily provokes the Giver not to give another time.

* * *

Blessed is the servant that treasures up for heaven (Mt. 6:20) the favors God extends to him, and that has no desire to disclose them to people in the hope of requital, because the Most High himself will make his works known to whomever he wishes.

Blessed the servant that keeps the secrets of the Lord carefully in his heart.

All
Praise Be
Yours, My
Lord,
Through All
That You
Have Made

Blessed Are You Among Women

Holy Virgin Mary, there was never anyone like
you born in the world among women! Daughter
and handmaiden of the most high King, our
Father in Heaven. Mother of our most holy Lord
Jesus Christ, Spouse of the Holy Spirit! With the
archangel St. Michael, and all the Virtues of
Heaven, and all the saints, pray for us at the
throne of your beloved most holy Son, our Lord
and Master.

* * *

O holy Mother, sweet and fair to see,
   for us beseech the King, your dearest Son,
   our Lord Jesus Christ,
   to death for us delivered:
That in his pitying clemency, and by virtue of
his most holy Incarnation, and bitter death
   He may pardon our sins. Amen.

Salutation of the Blessed Virgin

Hail, holy Lady,
  Most holy Queen,
  Mary, Mother of God,
  Ever Virgin;
Chosen by the most holy Father in heaven,
  Consecrated by him,
  With his most holy beloved Son
  And the Holy Spirit, the Comforter.
On you descended and in you still remains
  All the fulness of grace
  And every good.
Hail, his Palace.
Hail, his Tabernacle.
Hail, his Robe.
Hail, his Handmaid.
Hail, his Mother.
And Hail, all holy Virtues,
  Who, by the grace
  And inspiration of the Holy Spirit,
  Are poured into the hearts of the faithful
  So that, faithless no longer,
  They may be made faithful servants of God
  Through you.

Identifying the Poor With Christ

Strip the altar of the Blessed Virgin and take away its furnishings, if you have no other way to provide for the needy. Believe me, she will be more pleased to have her son's Gospel observed and her altar stripped, than to have her altar in trim and her son disregarded. The Lord will send someone to restore to his mother what she has lent us.

* * *

When you see a poor person, you ought to consider him in whose name he comes, Christ that is, who took our poverty and infirmity on himself. For such a person's infirmity and poverty is a kind of mirror for us, in which we ought to behold with pitying regard the infirmity and poverty which our Lord Jesus Christ bore in his person for our sake.

* * *

If you are so bountiful and polite toward people from whom you receive only a passing empty favor, it is no more than decent for you to be polite and bountiful toward God, who is so bounteous in giving to his poor.

The Canticle of Brother Sun I

Most high, all-powerful, all good, Lord!
   All praise is yours, all glory, all honour
   And all blessing.
To you, alone, Most High, do they belong.
   No mortal lips are worthy
   To pronounce your name.
All praise be yours, my Lord, through all that
you have made,
   And first my lord Brother Sun,
   Who brings the day; and light you give to
     us through him.
How beautiful is he, how radiant in all his
splendour!
   Of you, Most High, he bears the likeness.
All praise be yours, my Lord, through Sister
Moon and Stars;
   In the heavens you have made them, bright
   And precious and fair.
All praise be yours, my Lord, through
Brothers Wind and Air,
   All fair and stormy, all the weather's moods,
   By which you cherish all that you have made.
All praise by yours, my Lord, through Sister
Water,
   So useful, lowly, precious and pure.

The Canticle of Brother Sun II

All praise be yours, my Lord, through Brother
Fire,
    Through whom you brighten up the night.
    How beautiful is he, how gay! Full of power
      and strength.
All praise be yours, my Lord, through Sister
Earth, our mother,
    Who feeds us in her sovereignty and
      produces
    Various fruits with coloured flowers and
      herbs.
All praise be yours, my Lord, through those
who grant pardon
    For love of you; through those who endure
    Sickness and trial.
Happy those who endure in peace,
    By you, Most High, they will be crowned.
All praise be yours, my Lord, through Sister
Death,
    From whose embrace no mortal can escape.
Woe to those who die in mortal sin!
    Happy those she finds doing your will!
    The second death can do no harm to them.
Praise and bless my Lord, and give thanks,
    And serve him with great humility.

For Light of Sun and of Fire, Praise God!

In the morning when the sun rises, everybody ought to praise God, who created the sun for our benefit; through it our eyes get the light in daytime. At night, when darkness falls, everybody ought to praise God because of Brother Fire, through whom our eyes get light at night time.

For all of us are as it were blind, and the Lord with these two brothers of ours gives light to our eyes. Because of them in particular and all the creatures we make use of day by day, we ought to praise the Creator.

All You Winged Fowl,
Praise the Lord!

I believe our Lord Jesus Christ is pleased to have us stay on this solitary mountain, since our little brother and sister birds show such joy at our coming.

* * *

My sister swallows, it is time now for me to speak too, for up till now you have talked enough. Now you hear the word of God and remain silent and quiet until the word of the Lord has been taken care of.

* * *

My brother birds, you ought to praise your Creator mightily, and always love him. He has given you feathers to wear, and wings to fly, and whatever you have need of. God has made you noble among his creatures, and given you your home in the pure air, and though you neither sow nor reap, still without any trouble to you he protects and governs you.

All You Lowly Ones, Bless the Lord!

Sister Lark has a cowl like religious have, and a humble bird she is. She is happy going along the road to find a few kernels for herself. Even if she must find them amid dung, she picks them out and eats them. She praises the Lord very sweetly in her flight, like good religious, who spurn the earth, whose conversation is always in the heavens, and whose mind is always on the praises of God. Her garment (to wit: her feathers) resembles the ground, and she gives the religious an example not to wear choice and showy garments but such as are plain in price and color, just as the ground is plainer than the rest of the elements.

* * *

When I have speech with the emperor, I will beseech him to have a general ordinance issued that all who can afford it shall strew wheat and other grain along the roads, so that the little birds, especially our sister larks, may have an abundance on so solemn a feast day (Christmas).

* * *

. . . out of reverence for the Son of God, whom on that night the Blessed Virgin Mary laid down in a manger between ox and ass, whoever has an ox and an ass shall on that night supply them with the best of good feed; that likewise on that day all the poor ought to be given their fill of good victuals by the rich.

I Have
Done My
Duty.

hrist
Teach You
Yours.

Legacy of Francis

In that love which is God (1 Jn. 4:16), I, Brother
Francis, the least of your servants and worthy
only to kiss your feet, beg and implore all those
to whom this letter comes to hear these words
of our Lord Jesus Christ in a spirit of humility
and love, putting them into practice with all
gentleness and observing them perfectly. Those
who cannot read should have them read to
them often and keep them ever before their
eyes, by persevering in doing good to the last,
because they are *spirit and life* (Jn. 6:64). Those
who fail to do this shall be held to account for it
before the judgement-seat of Christ at the last
day. And may God, Father, Son, and Holy Spirit,
bless those who welcome them and grasp them
and send copies to others, if they persevere in
them to the last (Mt. 10:22).

* * *

And I strictly command all my brothers and
sisters, both clerical and lay, in obedience, not
to put glosses on the rule or on these words,
saying: they are to be understood thus: but, just
as the Lord has given it to me to speak and write
the rule and these words simply and purely,
thus simply and purely are you to understand
them and with holy practice to observe them to
the last.

Message of St. Francis to All

To all Christians, religious, clerics and layfolk, men and women; to everyone in the whole world, Brother Francis, their servant and subject, sends his humble respects, imploring for them true peace from heaven and sincere love in God.

I am the servant of all and so I am bound to wait upon everyone and make known to them the fragrant words of my Lord. Realizing, however, that because of my sickness and ill-health I cannot personally visit each one individually, I decided to send you a letter bringing a message with the words of our Lord Jesus Christ, who is the Word of the Father, and of the Holy Spirit, whose words are *spirit and life* (Jn. 6:64).

Bearing Much Fruit

Take courage, dearest brothers, and rejoice in the Lord. And do not be sad because you seem to be few, and do not let my plainness or yours discourage you; because, as the Lord has actually shown me, God is going to make us grow into a very great multitude and spread us out in numbers to the ends of the earth. For your benefit too I am forced to tell what I have seen, and yet I would much rather keep silent about it, if charity did not force me to relate it to you.

I have seen a great multitude of people coming to us and wishing to associate with us in our habit of holy conduct and our rule for a blessed religious life. Why, there is still in my ears the sound of them going and coming at the order of holy obedience. I have seen the roads so to say of every nation coming together hereabouts, filled with the multitude of them. Natives of France are coming, Spaniards hurrying along, Germans and Englishmen a-running, and a very great multitude of the various other tongues making haste.

To Suffer Out of Love of God

O Lord Jesus Christ, I entreat you to give me two graces before I die: first, that in my lifetime I may feel in body and soul as far as possible the pain you endured, dear Lord, in the hour of your most bitter suffering; and second, that I may feel in my heart as far as possible that excess of love by which you, O Son of God, were inflamed to undertake so cruel a suffering for us sinners.

* * *

I give you thanks, O Lord God, for these pains of mine, and I beg you, my Lord, add a hundredfold to them if it please you. It will be most agreeable to me that in afflicting me with pain you do not spare me. Fulfilling your holy will is more than ample comfort to me.

* * *

Suppose on account of need and poverty Brother Body cannot have what he needs in health and illness, or that it is not given to him when he asks another for it humbly and politely for the love of God, then let him suffer it patiently for the love of God, who likewise waited for someone to comfort him and found no one.

Such need borne with patience will be counted as martyrdom for him by the Lord. And because he did what he should, in humbly asking for what he needed, he is not guilty of sin though his body grow the more seriously ill for it.

Plea of Francis to Brother Fire During Temple Cauterization for His Eyes

My Brother Fire, that you might rival the beauty of all other things, the Most High created you vigorous, fair and useful. Be gracious to me at this moment, be courteous, for of old have I loved you in the Lord. I beg the great Lord, who created you, to temper your heat now, so that it will burn me gently enough to bear it.

* * *

Brothers, you with your faint spirits and weak hearts! What made you run away? I tell you candidly, I neither felt the heat of the fire nor any pain in my flesh.

Surrendering to God's Will for Me

God is mighty enough, should it please his will,
to drive off the cloud of darkness and extend
over us the blessing of light.

* * *

. . . that ever has been and remains more dear,
lovable and acceptable to me which it pleases
the Lord my God to have happen to me or con-
cerning me, and I desire always in everything to
be found altogether in harmony and compliance
with his will alone. But as for exchanging with
any kind of martyrdom, to bear this illness for
even three days would be more distressful; and I
am not saying this in estimation of the reward
but only of the distress the suffering causes.

* * *

The Lord, who comforts the afflicted, has never
left me without consolation. For look, after having no chance to listen to mortal lute play, I
have listened to a sweeter lute.

Welcome, Sister Death!

Please, O Lord, let the fiery, honeyed force of your love lap up my spirit from everything there is under heaven: so that I may die for love of love for you, who deigned to die for love of love for me.

* * *

I have done my duty. Christ teach you yours.

* * *

I wish to have no care about eating or drinking, brother. I put it all into your hands: if you give me anything, I will take it; if not, I will not ask for it.

* * *

When you see that I am being brought toward the end, lay me naked on the floor as you found me three days ago, and let me lie there in death for as long a time as it takes to walk a mile leisurely.

* * *

Tell me plainly, I say, and do not fear. For by the grace of God I am not a timid little heart, that I should fear death. The grace of the Holy Ghost helping, I am so at one with my Lord that I will not be sad over dying, nor rejoice any more over living longer. I will be equally pleased at life or death.

Blessing of St. Francis

And may whoever observes all this be filled in heaven with the blessing of the most high Father, and on earth with that of his beloved Son, together with the Holy Spirit, the Comforter, and all the powers of heaven and all the saints. And I, Brother Francis, your worthless servant, add my share internally and externally to that most holy blessing. Amen.

* * *

God bless and keep you.
May God smile on you, and be merciful to you;
May God turn his regard toward you
    and give you peace.
May God bless you . . .

Sources and Index

Adm: Admonitions of St. Francis
BC: Book of Conformities
BM: Bonaventure, *Major Legend*
1C: Celano, *First Life of St. Francis*
2C: Celano, *Second Life of St. Francis*
LAF: Letter to All the Faithful
LBL: Letter to Brother Leo
LF: *Little Flower of St. Francis*
LGC: Letter to General Chapter
LPO: Letter to Public Officials
LTC: *Legend of the Three Companions*
O: *Opuscula* (Collection of Written Works)
OP: Office of Passion
R: Rule of 1221
T: Testament of St. Francis
W: Wadding, *Opera Omnia*
(F): Fahy translation
(M): Meyer translation

49 2C 73 (M);
   LTC 9 (M)
50 R ch. 8 (F)
51 T (F)
52 LF 13 (M)
53 1C 84 (M);
   LGC (F)
54 Adm 1 (F)
55 Adm 1 (M)
56 T (F);
   2C 201 (M)
57 1C 16 (M)
59 1C 16 (M);
   R ch. 23 (F)
60 LGC (F)
61 Adm 13 (M);
   Adm 17 (M);
   Adm 23 (M)
62 Adm 9 (M);
   R ch. 22 (F)
63 LAF (M);
   LAF (F)
64 Adm 15 (M);
   Adm 21 (M);
   Adm 11 (F)
65 T (M);
   Adm 15 (F);
   LTC 14 (M)
66 Ascribed to St.
   Francis
67 LF (M)
69 LBL (F)
70 LAF (F);
   2C 196 (M)
71 R ch. 23 (F)
72 LAF (F); OP (M);
   R ch. 17 (F)
73 R ch. 23 #1 (F)
74 2C 99 (M);
   Adm 28 (M)

75 Cant. of Sun (F)
77 OP (M); W (M)
78 2C 198 (F)
79 2C 67 (M);
   MP 37 (M);
   LTC 1 (M)
80-81 (F)
82 MP 119 (M)
83 LF (M);
   1C 59 (M);
   1C 58 (M)
84 MP 113 (M);
   2C 200 (M);
   MP 114 (M)
85 2C 214 (M)
87 LAF (F); T (M)
88 LAF (F)
89 1C 27 (M)
90 LF (M);
   BM 14 (M);
   MP 97 (M)
91 2C 166 (M);
   2C 166 (M)
92 BM 5 (M);
   1C 107 (M);
   2C 126 (M)
93 O 125 (M);
   2C 214 (M);
   MP 107 (M);
   2C 217 (M);
   BC 12 (M)
94 T (F); LBL
   (quoting Num.
   6:24) (F)